EARTH'S LANDFORMS

VALLEYS

by Lisa J. Amstutz

Raintree is an imprint of Capstone Global Library Limited, a company incorporated in England and Wales having its registered office at 264 Banbury Road, Oxford, OX2 7DY – Registered company number: 6695582

www.raintree.co.uk
myorders@raintree.co.uk

Edited by Alesha Sullivan
Designed by Bobbie Nuytten
Original illustrations © Capstone Global Library Limited 2021
Picture research by Kelly Garvin
Production by Tori Abraham
Originated by Capstone Global Library Ltd

978 1 3982 0282 5 (hardback)
978 1 3982 0281 8 (paperback)

British Library Cataloguing in Publication Data
A full catalogue record for this book is available from the British Libr

Acknowledgements
We would like to thank the following for permission to reproduce photographs: Capstone Press/Karon Dubke, 20; Shutterstock: Amanda Mohler, 7, ArCaLu, 15, BerndBrueggemann, 9, canadastock, cover, Danilo Ascione, 19, Denis Belitsky, 17, ieuan, 16, Ivan Aleshin, 5, Kristi Blokhin, 11, Ruslan Suseynov, back cover, Stepo Dinaricus, 6, Thomas Dutour, 13

Every effort has been made to contact copyright holders of material reproduced in this book. Any omissions will be rectified in subsequent printings if notice is given to the publisher.

All the internet addresses (URLs) given in this book were valid at the time of going to press. However, due to the dynamic nature of the internet, some addresses may have changed, or sites may have changed or ceased to exist since publication. While the author and publisher regret any inconvenience this may cause readers, no responsibility for any such changes can be accepted by either the author or the publisher.

Printed and bound in India

Contents

Words in **bold** are in the glossary.

WHAT IS A VALLEY?

Have you ever seen a valley? A valley is a type of **landform**. It is lower than the land around it. Some valleys have mountains or hills on each side. Where the valley begins is called the head. The flattest part is called the floor.

HOW DO VALLEYS FORM?

Valleys are made in different ways. A river can make a valley. Water wears away the rock. These valleys can have **steep** sides. After many years, the valley gets wider and deeper.

The Grand Canyon is a large river
valley in North America. Canyons
are valleys with steep, rocky sides.

Large pieces of ice called **glaciers** can make valleys too. Over time, the ice gets heavy. It starts to slowly move over the ground. The ice cuts away rock. This type of valley is wide and flat.

TYPES OF VALLEYS

Rocky **plates** lie below the ground. They make up Earth's **crust**. Plates can push against each other. A piece of the crust is pushed down. It makes a ramp valley.

At other times plates move away from each other. This makes a wide, flat **rift** valley.

WHERE ARE VALLEYS FOUND?

There are valleys all over the world. The deepest valley is the Kali Gandaki Gorge in Asia. The Gandaki River runs along the bottom of the valley. In some places, it is said to be almost 6.4 kilometres (4 miles) deep.

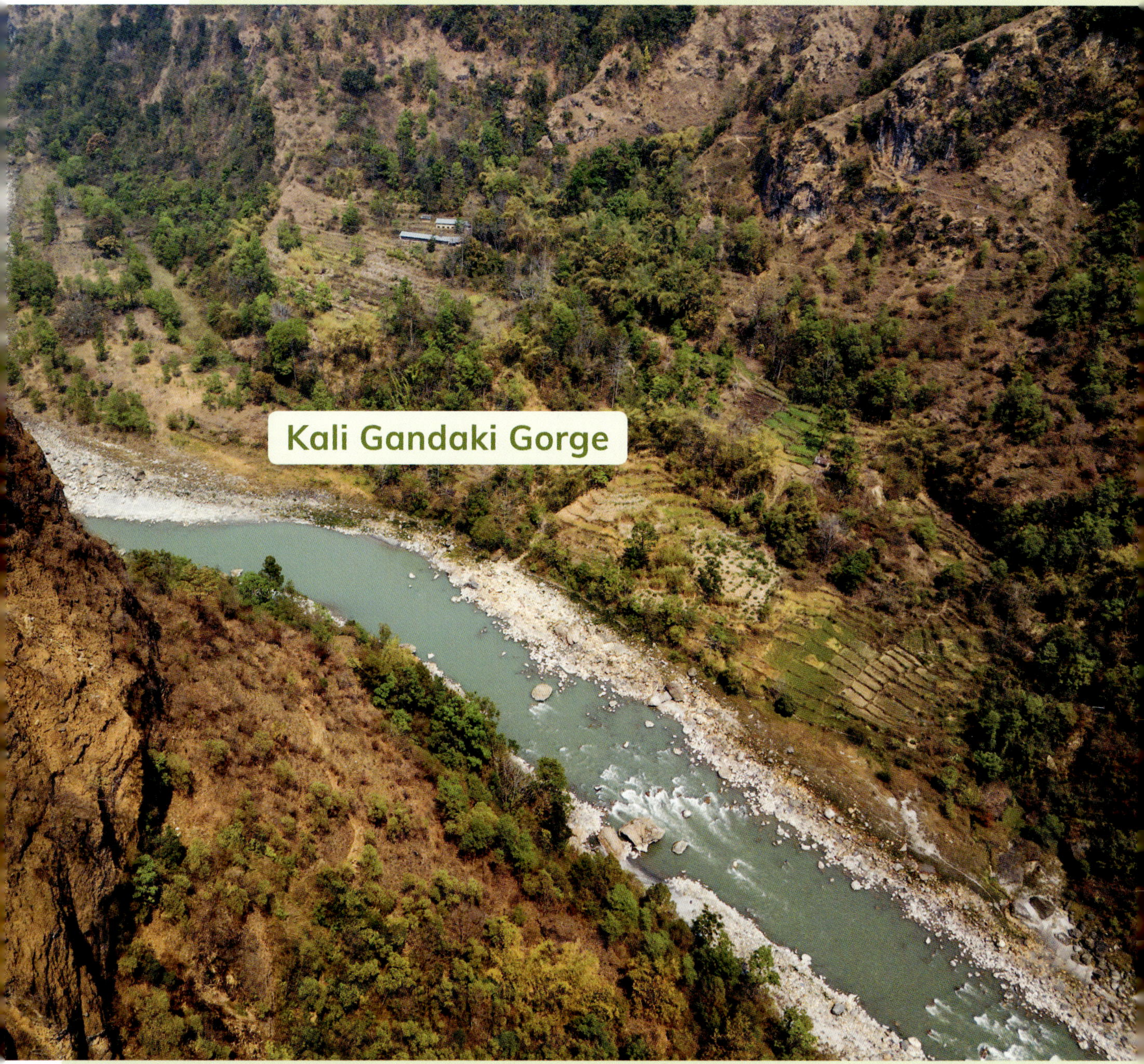
Kali Gandaki Gorge

Sometimes valleys are very long. The longest valley in the world is the Great Rift Valley in Africa. It is almost 6,440 km (4,000 miles) long. The giant rift was made by two plates moving away from each other.

WHAT LIVES IN A VALLEY?

Valleys are homes for many types of animals. Look up! Birds make nests in the trees on the **slopes**. Look down! Fish swim in the rivers and streams. Grasses and shrubs that do not need much sunlight grow here too.

Long ago, many people lived in valleys. They used the rivers to travel. Today, many people still live in valleys. They build towns and farms there. Would you like to live in a valley?

Make a valley

Use modelling clay to learn how glaciers shape valleys!

You'll need:

- modelling clay
- ice cube

Instructions:

1. Start with a mound of modelling clay. Press your finger into it to make a V-shaped valley.

2. Slide the ice cube through the base of the valley.

3. What happened to the valley's floor? What do you think would happen to the valley if the ice moved through it for many years?

Glossary

crust hard outer layer of Earth

glacier large, slow-moving sheet of ice

landform natural feature of the land

plate large sheet of rock that is a piece of Earth's crust

rift crack in Earth's surface

slope slanted surface; one end is higher than the other end on a slope

steep having a sharp slope or slant

Find out more

Books

DKfindout! Earth, DK (DK Children, 2017)

Earth's Landforms (Earth By Numbers),
Nancy Dickmann (Raintree, 2018)

Valleys (Learning About Landforms),
Ellen Labrecque (Raintree, 2015)

Websites

www.bbc.co.uk/bitesize/topics/z849q6f/articles/z7w8pg8
Learn more about rivers.

www.dkfindout.com/uk/earth/structure-earth
Find out more about the structure of Earth.

Index